Careers in the US Marine Corps

Other titles in the *Military Careers* series include:

Careers in the US Air Force
Careers in the US Army
Careers in the US Coast Guard
Careers in the US Navy
Careers in the US Special Forces

Careers in the US Marine Corps

Joanne Mattern

© 2016 ReferencePoint Press, Inc.
Printed in the United States

For more information, contact:
ReferencePoint Press, Inc.
PO Box 27779
San Diego, CA 92198
www.ReferencePointPress.com

LIBRARY OF CONGRESS CATALOGING-IN-PUBLICATION DATA

Mattern, Joanne, 1963-
    Careers in the US Marine Corps / by Joanne Mattern.
      pages cm. -- (Military careers)
    Includes bibliographical references and index.
      ISBN 978-1-60152-938-1 (hardback) -- ISBN 1-60152-938-4 (hardback) 1. United States. Marine Corps--Vocational guidance. I. Title.
      VE23.M392   2015
      359.9'602473--dc23
                                                            2015036327

Contents

The Mission of the Marine Corps

The US Marine Corps was founded in November 1775 when the Second Continental Congress passed a resolution calling for the creation of "two Battalions of Marines" to serve as landing forces with the navy. Early Marines distinguished themselves in several military operations, but the corps was disbanded after the Treaty of Paris was signed in 1783. The Marines reformed in 1798 and went on to serve and protect American interests around the world over the next 150 years, serving as far away as Africa and Asia and as close to home as Mexico.

However, it was not until the mid-twentieth century that the official mission of the US Marine Corps was established in the National Security Act of 1947. According to that act, Marines are "trained, organized, and equipped for offensive amphibious employment and as a force in readiness." This means that the Marines are designed to be a combined force of air, land, and sea assault, able to reach areas of conflict quickly by any means.

General Joseph F. Dunford, thirty-sixth commandant of the Marine Corps, described the mission of the Marines on the official Marine Corps website: "The Marine Corps is the Nation's expeditionary force in readiness. On a day-to-day basis, we are forward deployed, forward engaged, and prepared for crisis response. . . . The American people have come to expect us to do what must be done 'in any clime and place' and under any conditions. They expect us to respond quickly and to win."

Careers in the Marines

Approximately 178,000 people are part of the US Marine Corps. The Marines train every soldier to be a rifleman first, so all its members are ready for combat. However, there are many career opportunities in the Marines besides rifleman. Marine careers include three hundred different individual specialties. Each year, the Marine Corps recruits about forty thousand men and women to fill openings in its numerous career fields. Marines use every piece of modern war equipment. This means there are openings for pilots, sailors, tank crewmen, combat engineers, truck drivers and mechanics, weapons experts, and more. Marines work as radar and radio operators and operate sophisticated satellites and other equipment.

In addition to working with actual weapons and equipment, Marines are employed in numerous behind-the-scenes jobs. Some work to protect national security in their roles as intelligence specialists and linguists. Others hold administrative jobs or serve as police officers, meteorologists, food service workers, electrical engineers, lawyers, doctors, and much more.

Approximately 7 percent of Marines are women. Women traditionally have been barred from some combat careers, including positions in the infantry, artillery, and tanks units. However, the US Department of Defense (DOD) ordered all branches of the military to open all jobs to women beginning in January 2016. The DOD also gave military authorities the option to seek exemptions for certain jobs, including frontline combat jobs.

Career Paths for Officers and Enlisted Personnel

Like other branches of the US armed forces, Marines are divided into two basic groups: enlisted soldiers and officers. Everyone who joins the Marines has to decide which path is the best fit for his or her circumstances and career goals.

An enlisted soldier in the Marine Corps must be between ages seventeen and twenty-nine and be a US citizen or registered alien. Men and women who enlist in the Marines must be physically fit and meet strict physical, mental, and moral standards.

The Marine Corps also accepts candidates for officer training. An officer candidate must be between twenty and twenty-nine years old. To qualify as an officer, the candidate must have high moral standards.

US Armed Forces: Pay

In the US Armed Forces, pay for both enlisted personnel and officers depends on rank and years of service. Promotions depend on performance in addition to number of years served, with higher ranks translating to higher pay grades. The two graphs show monthly salaries commonly reached in the first four years of service.

Enlisted Pay

Monthly Salary Ranges for Enlisted Personnel with 0–4 Years in Service

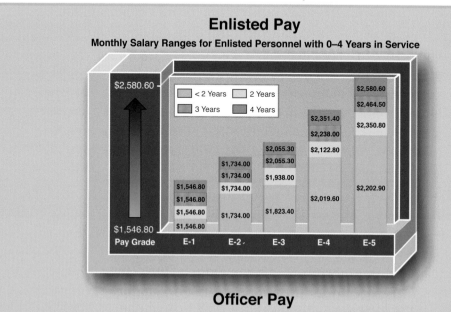

Officer Pay

Monthly Salary Ranges for Officers with 0–4 Years in Service

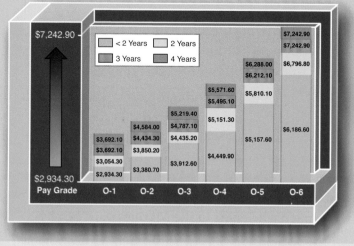

Note: Monthly salary ranges in both graphs are based on enlisted and officer pay scales effective January 1, 2015. The pay scales described here do not take into account the value of health benefits or housing and other allowances.

Source: Defense Finance and Accounting Service, "Military Pay Charts, 1949 to 2015," December 23, 2014. www.dfas.mil/militarymembers/payentitlements/military-pay-charts.html.

He or she must also have a four-year college degree, be physically fit, and have demonstrated leadership potential. In addition, applicants for officer training must be US citizens. They have to pass the initial Marine Corps physical fitness test. In addition, they must take either the SAT, ACT, or Armed Services Vocational Aptitude Battery (ASVAB) and score a minimum of 1,000 combined verbal and math on the SAT, 22 on the ACT, and 115 on the electronics repair composite of the ASVAB. Students who wish to become officers can enroll in a Reserve Officer Training Corps (ROTC) or Naval Reserve Officer Training Corps (NROTC) program during college, which provides military training and leads to a commissioned officer position upon graduation. (Some high schools also offer Junior ROTC programs.)

Enlisted Marines may also become officers through a program called the Marine Corps Enlisted Commissioning Education Program, or MECEP. MECEP offers qualified Marines the chance to go to a four-year college full time while maintaining active duty status and pay. This program is open to all active duty or active reserve Marines who meet the eligibility requirements. Participants are selected based on an individual's potential, service record, previous academic record, and evidence of career and academic self-improvement. A candidate who is selected for MECEP will attend a ten-week Officer Candidate School course. After completing that course, the Marine will attend a university or college that offers an NROTC program. After completing a degree, he or she will be commissioned as a second lieutenant.

Why Become a Marine?

The motto of the Marine Corps is *Semper Fidelis*, which is Latin for "always faithful." Marines are often the first US military force to arrive in a war zone, and members of the corps take great pride in their bravery and can-do attitude. Members of the corps often say that "there is no such thing as an ex-Marine" and are fanatically proud of their efforts and abilities.

Marines are unique among the armed forces in that they can serve in many different capacities. Marines serve on US Navy ships, protect naval bases, guard US embassies, and provide a quick strike force that is always ready to protect US interests around the globe. This makes the Marines a dynamic force that can deploy anywhere in the world on a moment's notice. Unlike the other armed forces, which focus on one approach to battle, Marines are trained to attack from the land, the sea, and the air.

Serving in the Marine Corps requires a special kind of individual, but service can provide a fulfilling career and unsurpassed opportunities. Those who are disciplined, determined, and want to become part of a very special community might find unusual and unique paths for personal growth and career achievement in in the Marine Corps.

Avionics Technician

What Does an Avionics Technician Do?

The Marine Corps is a combined arms force that includes coverage of air, land, and sea. It was the introduction of air transportation that allowed the Marines to become a swift reaction force, able to arrive in a combat situation very quickly. Marine aviation makes it possible for troops to get right into battle, as well as provide support for ground and naval forces.

The Marine Corps maintains its strong air power by operating one of the largest aviation fleets in the world. This fleet includes a variety of aircraft, including jets, helicopters, cargo planes, and drones. Each Marine squadron typically includes four to twenty-four aircraft. Since the corps includes more than eighty squadrons, that means there are hundreds of Marine Corps aircraft in service. These aircraft have been proven time and time again in warfare. In his book *Coalition Air Warfare in the Korean War, 1950–1953*, author Jacob Neufeld quotes Colonel Paul L. Freeman, a US Army commander, who registered his awe at the Marine Corps' air defense system during that conflict. "The Marines on our left

At a Glance:

Avionics Technician

Minimum Educational Requirements
High school diploma or the equivalent

Personal Qualities
Detail oriented, good problem solver, able to work in a team

Certification and Licensing
FAA airframe and powerplant license

Working Conditions
In airplane hangars or repair stations

Salary Range
Monthly salary depends on pay grade and years of service

Future Job Outlook
Average growth rate through 2022

A Marine Corps avionics technician checks wiring on a Huey helicopter aboard the aircraft carrier USS Iwo Jima. *Avionics technicians routinely conduct flight maintenance on aircraft electronic systems.*

were a sight to behold," Freeman wrote. "They had squadrons of air in direct support. They used it like artillery. We just have to have air support like that or we might as well disband and join the Marines."

All of these aircraft require careful maintenance to stay in top condition. That's where avionics technicians enter the picture. Avionics technicians are responsible for all the electronic parts of an aircraft. Marines in the avionics field install, remove, inspect, test, maintain, and repair all aviation weapons and electrical systems. They also inspect and maintain communications, radar, and navigation systems. Avionics technicians develop, install, repair, test, and service electronic equipment for airplanes. They may work on devices such as radios, transmitters, autopilot technology, navigation equipment, weather detection equipment, flight recorders, and flight control equipment.

Avionics technicians have a wide variety of responsibilities. They perform preflight checks and maintenance, and all inspections and repairs following each mission. They are responsible for maintaining electronic equipment, troubleshooting and solving problems, repairing or replacing faulty equipment, rewiring and replacing electrical circuits, upgrading electrical equipment, and testing equipment to make sure it is working properly.

Military aircraft could not fly without avionics technicians. In addition to keeping aviation equipment working properly, an avionics technician's work ensures the safety of all the people on board that plane. Sergeant Jeffrey Grant, an avionics supervisor who served on board the aircraft carrier USS *Enterprise* in 2012, explained in an article titled "Avionics Marines Keep Bolts Striking" on the official Marine Corps website that "issues we face at our level can be caused from bad wires, defective circuit boards, failing radar systems, and much more, which all need to be tested. The work we do in avionics makes flight operations successful because if we didn't do our job to fix electronic components, the overall mission of Marine Corps aviation could be affected."

Some Marine Corps avionics technicians train on a variety of systems, whereas others specialize. There are several avionic specialties within the Marines. For example, an aircraft communications/navigation/electrical/systems technician supports all electrical systems, components, and ancillary equipment on a specific type of plane. An aircraft electronic countermeasures systems technician operates the defensive systems such as jammers and missiles, and an avionics test set technician inspects, tests, maintains, and repairs aircraft weapon systems. Technicians usually work in teams, with each member specializing in one or two areas such as navigational equipment or communications and radar systems. Some avionics technicians might work on specific equipment such as an airplane or helicopter, whereas others are trained to work on a wide variety of machines.

How Do You Become an Avionics Technician?

Education

A high school diploma or the equivalent is required to enter the Marine Corps. High school students who have an interest in working as avionics technicians should take courses in math, computers, and, if available, electrical engineering. Students may also wish to take a vocational electrical repair course. Once a student has joined the Marines, he or she will take the Armed Services Vocational Aptitude Battery, or ASVAB, to determine what useful skills he or she possesses.

After completing sixteen weeks of basic training, or boot camp, most Marines interested in becoming avionics technicians train for this specialty by taking classes at a Marine base. Job training consists of classroom instruction, including practice in repairing avionics systems. Training length varies depending on specialty. Further training occurs on the job and through advanced courses that are also offered on Marine bases. Course content typically includes electronics and electrical theory, troubleshooting procedures, installation techniques, and avionics and electrical system maintenance.

Avionics technicians work with a variety of different tools. Technicians use hand tools such as wrenches, screwdrivers, and soldering irons. Technicians may also use instruments such as oscilloscopes or voltmeters to test electronic equipment. At times they may remove a piece of equipment from an aircraft and examine it under an X-ray or magnetic inspection machine. Avionics technicians also use computers on a regular basis and know how to read diagrams and blueprints. Therefore, avionics technicians must acquire skills in using a variety of equipment to perform their duties.

Certification and Licensing

In addition to the courses required by the Marines, the Federal Aviation Administration (FAA) requires all avionics technicians to be certified by taking courses approved by the FAA, including the licensing course for airframe and powerplant. The FAA also requires avionics technicians to have current experience in order to remain certified.

Volunteer Work and Internships

Before entering the Marine Corps, students may benefit from finding volunteer work or internships in the avionics field. Students can look for opportunities at local airports, electronic testing and repair facilities, or factories that produce aviation electronic equipment.

Skills and Personality

An avionics technician must be detail oriented and good at identifying and solving problems. He or she must be able to work under pressure and as part of a team. Communication with other team members is an essential part of the job, since technicians and engineers work together to diagnose and repair issues. Avionics technicians should be able to troubleshoot easily and to identify problems and figure out their solutions quickly and competently. Critical-thinking skills are important in this field, as well as being a good listener in order to gather clues and identify what is causing a problem.

It is important for an avionics technician to have strong math and computer skills. He or she should also be interested in electronics. Because they work with electronics, avionics technicians should have strong mechanical skills and be good at figuring out how things work. Technicians should be good at working with their hands and have good eye-hand coordination. Technicians must also have good eyesight and perfect color vision.

An avionics technician must be good at time management. Aircraft are inspected and maintained on a specific schedule set out by the FAA. Maintenance schedules vary according to the number of hours an individual aircraft has flown or the number of days since its last inspection. In addition to following regular maintenance schedules, avionics technicians may also inspect or repair a part after they receive a complaint from a pilot or other aircraft personnel.

In addition to their repairing and maintenance tasks, avionics technicians must also keep meticulous records of their work. They note the inspections and repairs they have made and describe how they corrected a problem. These records help maintain safety standards and track problems.

Technicians work under a great deal of pressure. They must meet tight deadlines and stay on schedule without rushing through their work or cutting corners. It is essential that avionics technicians be thorough, meticulous, and careful to make sure that the aircraft they are working on is safe to fly.

On the Job

Working Conditions

Avionics technicians may work in a hangar or a repair station shop. Technicians may also work with engineers to inspect or repair electrical equipment. Sometimes they work at tool benches, but often they must get inside aircraft to wire systems or fit parts. These places are often small and confining, so technicians must be nimble to do their jobs. Avionics technicians may also be called on to work on ladders or scaffolds, standing for long periods, to reach parts of larger aircraft. The job can be fatiguing, but most technicians enjoy working on the unique, high-tech aircraft.

Earnings

As of June 2015, the average salary for an avionics technician in the Marine Corps was $44,394 per year. Avionics technicians in the military also receive other benefits such as health insurance for themselves and their family and paid leave and time off. Marines also receive free housing on base or a housing allowance if they live off base.

Opportunities for Advancement

As with the other armed services, advancement in the Marines depends on an individual's performance and time served. As individuals gain more experience, they may go up in rank and receive greater opportunities.

As a Marine avionics technician is promoted, he or she will take on additional responsibility for repair and administrative requirements for multiple systems. An individual can advance to a supervisory position or choose to become an officer if he or she meets the educational and aptitude qualifications.

Even as they advance, it is important for avionics technicians to stay up-to-date in their field. Electronic equipment is constantly being upgraded and improved, and avionics technicians must keep up with these changes. Technicians need to read technical articles and are required to take refresher courses to stay current.

What Is the Future Outlook for Avionics Technicians?

The Marine Corps operates one of the largest aviation fleets in the world, so there is a great demand for avionics technicians and other specialized aviation support roles such as aircraft maintenance staff and air traffic controllers. According to the Bureau of Labor Statistics, opportunities in the armed forces should remain good through the year 2022. The Marines, like other branches of the armed services, constantly need to fill both entry-level and professional positions as members are promoted through the ranks, leave the service, or retire.

What Are Employment Prospects in the Civilian World?

Avionics technicians have many job opportunities in the civilian world. Civilian avionics technicians are employed by commercial airlines, aircraft manufacturers, aviation repair stations, avionics equipment manufacturers, and air transport companies. In addition, the federal government also employs many avionics technicians.

With further education, avionics technicians are well positioned to move into other aviation-related jobs such as aerospace engineers or aircraft inspectors. They may also move into other occupations that require familiarity and skills with electronic equipment, such as electronic engineering technicians, electrical and electronic installers, electrical and electronic inspectors, or general electrical or electronics careers.

Combat Engineer

What Does a Combat Engineer Do?

Engineers are essential members of the Marines Corps. Their job has two focuses: building and destroying. In general, a combat engineer's purpose is to support fellow Marines and other friendly forces by building structures to make movement easier and to destroy structures to make it harder for the enemy to move freely or stage an attack.

When Marines advance into war-torn areas, they often need to build roads or structures or keep local services such as power plants and water-treatment facilities functioning. Working alongside military construction crews, combat engineers may take part in these efforts. In Iraq and Afghanistan, for example, combat engineers have rebuilt vital facilities such as schools and clinics to help local populations. Marine Corps engineers repair, construct, and fabricate any infrastructure the Marines need to perform their duties, and they may work with local engineers to restore infrastructure damaged in combat.

Combat engineering includes a great deal of construction, so these soldiers will train in construction trades such as carpentry, masonry, and building. Engineers will also be asked to construct and remodel a

At a Glance:
Combat Engineer

Minimum Educational Requirements
High school diploma or the equivalent

Personal Qualities
Patient, detail oriented, confident, able to handle stress and work in a team

Working Conditions
On a base or in the field, possibly in a combat situation

Salary Range
Monthly salary depends on pay grade and years of service

Future Job Outlook
Average growth rate through 2022

variety of different structures, so they must be able to understand engineering and construction plans and work quickly to build or repair necessary structures. Many are trained to operate heavy construction equipment to get big projects done.

Besides aiding in tending or constructing needed infrastructure, combat engineers also have roles to play on the battlefield. A combat engineer platoon supports ground forces by getting through enemy obstacles and minefields, building causeways and bunkers for its own troops, and erecting roads, bridges, and airstrips to keep allied forces moving. Combat engineers may even perform "route reconnaissance" to figure out the best ways to move from one place to another quickly and safely. These soldiers truly function as jacks-of-all-trades. In their offensive role, combat engineers are demolition experts as well. A Marine Corps adage asserts that combat engineers are to be relied on to demolish a target "when it absolutely must be destroyed overnight." That is, along with building necessary structures, combat engineers also blow them up. The Marines turn to combat engineers to destroy enemy buildings, fortresses, bridges, ammunition storage buildings, and other structures. Therefore, handling and setting explosives are vital parts of a combat engineer's job. On the Marine Corps website, www.marines.com, Captain Michael Baliko, a combat engineer officer, describes the dual nature of the Marine Corps combat engineer's job. "I basically lead my Marines to blow things up well and to build 'em as well."

Combat engineers work with different groups or battalions. Sometimes their role is to ensure that runways are safe and accessible for military aircraft. Other times they are tasked with clearing a path for fellow Marines and other US forces as they make their way to a designated location in a war zone. Baliko says this can involve "exploding things, blowing things up, blowing up obstacles, offensively striking the enemy if we have to. But primarily as engineer support battalion Marines, we're looking at mobility, so, freeing up that roadway if there are obstacles. We use demolitions to get rid of whatever obstacles or debris there are that impede the infantry or Marine forces from getting from Point A to Point B."

The job of combat engineer officer involves a great deal of planning, especially to prepare for future missions. Baliko continues,

During a demolitions exercise, a Marine Corps combat engineer pulls the timed fuse on a charge to destroy a wire trap. Combat engineers destroy obstacles and build structures to aid movement by US forces and impede enemy attacks.

"You're always setting the next mission as the highest priority. You're looking forward to prepare and plan as much as you possibly can, and then you're also executing. This past deployment, I was the convoy commander, so I'd lead the entire convoy of logistical vehicles and tactical vehicles from Point A to Point B, wherever it may be in Iraq. And as soon as that piece is over, as soon as the convoy's over, once my Marines hit the deck and we're at that location, I then lead to the actual mission, the mission commander, and take that seat where I lead all my Marines in executing the mission that we've transited out there to execute."

Combat engineers do not just remove debris and other obstacles. Another of the major duties of a Marine Corps combat engineer is to remove enemy mines. To do this, engineers might use handheld electronic tools to detect a mine's location, then disable the mine or destroy it by blowing it up. Alternatively, combat engineers might employ mine-clearing vehicles to do the job. It is the combat engineer's job to remove any and all dangerous obstacles the Marines come across in battle or behind the lines.

Like all Marines, combat engineers must be ready to move out at a moment's notice and rapidly complete their missions. They may be deployed in war zones or in areas that have been affected by natural disasters such as hurricanes, lending their construction skills to those in need. They can work anywhere from rural areas to major cities, performing the numerous jobs they are trained to do.

How Do You Become a Combat Engineer?

Education

A high school diploma or the equivalent is required to enter the Marine Corps. Some combat engineers already have college degrees in engineering when they join the Marines. Others are trained through Marine Corps courses.

High school students who have an interest in working as combat engineers should take courses in math, physics, and, if available, mechanical engineering. They may also study drafting or computer-assisted design. Students may also wish to take a vocational course in a construction-related field. Once a student has joined the Marines, he or she will take the Armed Services Vocational Aptitude Battery, or ASVAB. A recruit who wishes to serve as a combat engineer will need a high score in the mechanical maintenance portion of the ASVAB.

After joining the Marine Corps and completing sixteen weeks of basic training, or boot camp, Marines in the engineering occupational field will complete a specialty course dependent on their military occupational specialty (MOS) code. Courses include the Basic Combat Engineer Course, the Engineer Equipment Operator Course, and the Basic Metal Workers Course. Once an MOS is determined, a Marine combat engineer may be assigned to a combat engineer battalion, an engineer support battalion, or another battalion.

Marine Volunteer Work and Internships

Before entering the Marine Corps, students may benefit from finding volunteer work or internships in the construction field. Students can look for opportunities with local builders or unions specializing in construction trades.

Skills and Personality

A combat engineer must be able to work under pressure. He or she will often be in dangerous situations, such as active combat, war zones, or areas that have suffered a natural disaster. An engineer should be flexible and able to work in different physical and mental situations. He or she should be able to work as part of a team and have good communication skills. Critical-thinking skills are important in this field, as well as being a good listener in order to size up a job and take action as quickly and safely as possible.

It is important for a combat engineer to be prepared to work with dangerous equipment. During demolition jobs, an engineer will use explosives and other volatile materials to blow things up. Combat engineers are also trained to deactivate and remove mines, so they need nerves of steel and a lot of courage to do this extremely dangerous job.

Because they also work in construction, combat engineers should have strong mechanical skills and be good at figuring out how to build things. They should be able to understand and interpret building plans and blueprints, as well as be able to build structures under a lot of time pressure. Engineers should also be good at working with their hands and have good eye-hand coordination. They must also have excellent vision and hearing.

On missions, they must meet tight deadlines and stay on schedule while putting safety first. Their actions improve the battlefield conditions for their fellow soldiers, and their construction and maintenance work can benefit the lives of civilians as well.

On the Job

Working Conditions

Combat engineers frequently work in extremely stressful conditions in the field. Many are deployed on combat missions, which places them in war zones and on battlefields. Combat engineers often work in difficult physical locations, such as bombed-out cities or remote locations.

During peacetime, combat engineers may be sent around the world to help victims of natural disasters. They may face difficult conditions as they work to restore basic and necessary services by rebuilding power plants, water treatment plants, roads, and other essential infrastructure. Despite these conditions, many combat engineers take a great deal of satisfaction in their work, knowing that they are keeping fellow soldiers and civilians safe and helping people resume a normal life after war or disaster.

Earnings

As of June 2015, salaries for a combat engineer in the Marine Corps ranged from $31,089 to $79,000, with an average salary of $53,201 per year. Pay varies depending on rank, experience, location, and other factors. Military personnel also receive other benefits such as health insurance for themselves and their family and paid leave and time off. Marines also receive free housing on base or a housing allowance if they live off base.

Opportunities for Advancement

As with the other armed services, advancement in the Marines depends on an individual's performance and time served. As individuals gain more experience, they may go up in rank and receive greater opportunities. Enlisted Marines may also become officers, which will increase their opportunities.

As a combat engineer is promoted, he or she will take on additional responsibilities. An engineer in a supervisory position will manage other engineers or head a team working on a specific goal.

What Is the Future Outlook for Combat Engineers?

Since the Marine Corps is often the first branch of the armed forces to hit the ground during military operations, there is a great demand for engineers who can construct and repair essential buildings and also demolish structures used by enemy forces. For this reason, combat engineers should remain a vital part of the Marines in the future.

According to the Bureau of Labor Statistics, opportunities in the armed forces should remain good through the year 2022. The Marines, like other branches of the armed services, constantly need to fill both entry-level and professional positions as members are promoted through the ranks, leave the service, or retire.

What Are Employment Prospects in the Civilian World?

Combat engineers have many job opportunities in the civilian world. Because of their excellent training, they can work in a variety of construction fields or do demolition work. Some find work with other military contractors or go to work as construction specialists for organizations that work in communities needing basic infrastructure, such as hospitals or public-works projects. Engineers with advanced degrees can also find work as civil engineers, mechanical engineers, or other positions in the engineering field, or move into commercial or residential architecture.

Field Artillery Cannoneer

What Does a Field Artillery Cannoneer Do?

The Marines are a quick-reaction force meant to be in the thick of battle. While Marine foot soldiers deploy on the front lines, they receive artillery support from their comrades positioned well behind those lines. "When infantrymen are in a firefight, they can count on the supporting fire of an artillery battery when they are suppressed by the enemy," says field artillery cannoneer lance corporal Philip Morrill in an article titled "Artillery Marines Force of Destruction When in Synch." Artillery support is a major part of the Marine Corps' strength, and the field artillery cannoneers who operate these cannons are valuable members of any division.

Whether the Marine Corps is taking part in field exercises for training or actually deployed in a combat situation, its artillery is one of the keys to success in battle, and the men and women who operate the guns are vital to that success. A field artillery cannoneer is part of a field artillery howitzer battery. A howitzer is a type of cannon that has a relatively short barrel

At a Glance:
Field Artillery Cannoneer

Minimum Educational Requirements
High school diploma or the equivalent

Personal Qualities
Patient, detail oriented, thorough, able to work as part of a team

Working Conditions
On a base or in the field, possibly in a combat situation

Salary Range
Monthly salary depends on pay grade and years of service

Future Job Outlook
Average growth rate through 2022

25

A Marine Corps field artillery cannoneer cleans the breach of a howitzer during a training exercise. Cannoneers operate and maintain artillery such howitzers, which are capable of firing high-explosive satellite-guided rounds.

that can propel projectiles very high into the air. The Marine Corps began using the M777 howitzer in 2005. At a weight of just under 10,000 pounds (4,218 kg), the M777 is 42 percent lighter than previous howitzers, making it easier to transport and maneuver in the field. Some field artillery cannoneers also operate the High Mobility Artillery Rocket System, or HIMARS. This system can fire multiple rockets over a long range with excellent precision. The howitzers, rocket batteries, and their operators can be quickly deployed to support any action.

Field artillery cannoneers have many responsibilities, all connected with making sure artillery pieces and equipment are maintained and ready to be used. One of a cannoneer's main jobs is to prepare artillery pieces and equipment for movement, combat, and firing. Field artillery cannoneers learn how to take apart and put together artillery equipment. They inspect and prepare ammunition for firing, and they perform the various jobs necessary for a weapon to fire successfully. These tasks include making sure the elevation and aim of the weapon is correct so the projectile will avoid any obstacles between the weapon and its target. Field artillery cannoneers are also responsible for loading the weapon and handling ammunition. They also inspect the ammunition to make sure it is the right kind for the weapon and that it is not defective in any way.

Field artillery cannoneers also perform preventive maintenance and clean artillery pieces and equipment so they are able to perform at peak efficiency. They make routine tests and authorize repairs to equipment. Cannoneers may also be responsible for setting up camouflage to hide their guns, protecting equipment from chemical warfare agents, and constructing field fortifications.

Howitzers and rocket batteries are often transported to field exercises and battle sites by truck. For this reason, a field artillery cannoneer may also be trained to drive the huge, 7-ton (6.4-metric-ton) trucks that bring these big weapons where they need to be. Overall, the cannon crews are responsible for moving their howitzers to designated sites, unlimbering them from transport vehicles, preparing them for targeting and firing, and finally shooting them off on command.

How Do You Become a Field Artillery Cannoneer?

Education

A high school diploma or the equivalent is required to enter the Marine Corps. High school students who have an interest in working as field artillery cannoneers should take courses in math and physics because setting targeting trajectories will rely on such knowledge. Once a student has joined the Marines, he or she will take the Armed Services Vocational Aptitude Battery to determine the jobs for which he or she is eligible.

After joining the Marine Corps and completing sixteen weeks of basic training, or boot camp, most field artillery cannoneers travel to Fort Sill in Oklahoma to train for this specialty. Fort Sill offers several training courses, including the Cannon Crewman Course, which lasts five weeks and is designed to train entry-level Marines. This course is a combination of classroom instruction and hands-on practical application in the field.

Field artillery cannoneers may also take a two-and-a-half-week HIMARS Crewman Course to learn how to operate the HIMARS. There is also a Cannon Crewman Advanced Course, which lasts six weeks. This course is designed to train senior cannoneers in the grades of staff sergeant through master gunnery sergeant.

Skills and Personality

Field artillery cannoneers work with others, so they must be able to work under pressure and as part of a team. Communication with other team members is an essential part of the job. In an article titled "Artillery Marines Force of Destruction when in Synch," which appeared on the official Marine Corps website in 2013, Corporal Patrick Hickey, an assistant section chief with India Battery, First Battalion, Eleventh Marine Regiment, explains his job during a live-fire training exercise at Camp Pendleton. He says:

> There are seven field artillery cannoneer positions and one section chief. The section chief oversees all the Marines working with the howitzer. He verifies all incoming fire mission data used to confirm target information and ensures the correct ammunition is being loaded into the gun. He must be able to stand back and observe everything that happens and what everyone is doing. He makes sure everything runs smoothly.

Meanwhile, the cannoneers each have a specific job to do. Corporal Philip Morrill, also of the India Battery, explains that cannoneer one's job is to open the loading tray for a round to be loaded into the howitzer. Cannoneer two places the rounds and charges onto the loading tray of the howitzer and waits for the chief to verify the correct round and charge issued. Then cannoneer one pulls the lanyard, which fires the cannon. After firing each round, cannoneer two runs a moist swab inside the cannon to cool it down so the barrel doesn't melt or jam. Cannoneer three assists cannoneer two by passing rounds and charges from the top of the nearby ammunition stack to the gun. Cannoneer four makes sure there are enough rounds unloaded off the battery's ammunition truck and that each round has the proper fuse.

Because they are responsible for maintaining and repairing weapons, field artillery cannoneers should be able to troubleshoot easily, identify problems, and figure out their solutions quickly and competently. Critical-thinking skills are important in this field.

A field artillery cannoneer needs to put expensive equipment together quickly, competently, and safely. For this reason, it is important for a field artillery cannoneer to have strong mechanical skills. Cannoneers work with their hands on a daily basis and should be skilled in putting things together and performing maintenance and repair work. Strong attention to detail is also very important.

Physical strength is also important for a field artillery cannoneer. Howitzers and other cannons are large, heavy pieces of equipment. Working with this equipment requires physical strength, especially in the arms and legs. Cannoneers should strive to be physically fit and be willing to exercise to maintain their body strength and flexibility.

In addition, field artillery cannoneers often work under harsh field conditions, so they should be able to withstand rough sleeping conditions, long work hours, and stressful physical conditions. They may be asked to work under a great deal of pressure, especially in training exercises or combat situations.

On the Job

Working Conditions

Field artillery cannoneers may work on a base or in the field. When they are on base, cannoneers work in a gun park, a large lot with an overhead cover. Cannoneers inspect, repair, and maintain their equipment in this covered area. When out on the field for exercises or for combat, cannoneers are outside almost all of the time. They must deal with all kinds of weather conditions and get used to sleeping out in the open.

Live-fire training exercises are an important part of a cannoneer's training. These exercises allow the Marines to fire rockets and shells in a controlled environment so they can maintain and strengthen their skills to be more effective in combat. In the Marine Corps website article titled "5/11 Marines Deliver Long-Range Destruction," Sergeant Caleb Staats, a rocket launcher chief with Battery Q at Camp Pendleton, California, explains that live-fire exercises are an essential part of being as prepared as possible when deployed. "Firing a rocket is a very exhilarating and nerve-wracking experience," said Staats. "If we don't keep doing training exercises and running through the procedures regularly, Marines can forget how it feels when you actually fire, causing them to be disoriented when it comes time to do what we are tasked to do in combat."

Earnings

As of June 2015, salaries for a field artillery cannoneer in the Marine Corps range between $32,000 and $48,000 per year. Field artillery cannoneers in the military also receive other benefits such as health insurance for themselves and their family and paid leave and time off. Marines also receive free housing on base or a housing allowance if they live off base.

Opportunities for Advancement

As with the other armed services, advancement in the Marines depends on an individual's performance and time served. As individuals gain more experience, they may go up in rank and receive greater opportunities. Field artillery cannoneers may advance by gaining more experience or training to be an officer. As field artillery cannoneers are promoted, they will take on additional responsibilities such as supervising crews.

What Is the Future Outlook for Field Artillery Cannoneers?

Since the Marine Corps is in the business of providing trained personnel for combat situations, the outlook for field artillery cannoneers should remain high. These skilled forces are needed in almost any battle situation, and their experience and training in weaponry should make this a much-needed position in the Marines.

What Are Employment Prospects in the Civilian World?

Although there is little use for operating and maintaining cannons in the civilian world, field artillery cannoneers may find employment at a weapons manufacturer or a weapons-based business. They may also find work with a government or private contractor working on building, testing, or maintaining artillery and other combat weaponry.

However, many employers prize workers who have strong senses of discipline and responsibility, which are values that any Marine veteran should possess. Field artillery cannoneers should be able to transfer their Marine training and values into various jobs in the civilian world, even if they are not strictly related to weapons training.

Intelligence Specialist

What Does an Intelligence Specialist Do?

In the military, *intelligence* is the term for gathering information about other countries, enemy forces, or people in the area where troops are stationed. The job of an intelligence specialist is to find out everything he or she can about the people living in areas where Marines are operating or might be deployed.

At a Glance:

Intelligence Specialist

Minimum Educational Requirements
High school diploma or the equivalent

Personal Qualities
Excellent communicator, able to build relationships with people, good problem solver

Certification and Licensing
Security clearance

Working Conditions
In an office on base or in the field

Salary Range
Monthly salary depends on pay grade and years of service

Future Job Outlook
Better-than-average growth rate through 2022

Intelligence specialists gather information in many different ways. Some study maps and satellite images to understand how another country is deploying its armed forces or whether a country is building munitions factories or other facilities to wage war. Other intelligence specialists intercept electronic signals and communications to find out what enemy officers or government officials are saying to each other.

In a forum post on the Military.com website, a former intelligence specialist described his job as being a "jack-of-all-trades for the intel field." During his time in the service, he performed a variety of jobs, including conducting surveillance on protesters outside a military base, photographing weapons caches, and transporting classified materials to officers in other camps. He also served on military bases as a training officer. This specialist explains, "This job requires a lot of time for research, writing, studying, and thinking."

Still other intelligence specialists interact with people in foreign communities. For example, an intelligence specialist may talk to residents of a country where the Marines are conducting operations. The specialists will become part of the local community and observe how residents live. Creating these bonds allows specialists to learn more about enemy warlords or agents and gain behind-the-scenes information about the enemy's plans or goals. This type of intelligence is called human intelligence. It provides information troops cannot get in any other way. In an article titled "Corps Ramps Up Recruiting for Lucrative, Unconventional Intel Jobs," written by Gina Harkins and published on the *Marine Corps Times* website in 2013, Colonel Andrew Moyer, who serves as chief of staff for the director of Marine Corps Intelligence at the Pentagon, explains, "The nature of human intelligence is such that it provides context to information you just can't get through other means. Through signals intelligence, you can derive certain things and through geospatial intelligence, you can derive certain things. But it's very difficult to put those things into context." Adding personal observations, as is done by human intelligence officers, helps provide information to fill in the blanks left by other intelligence sources.

Counterintelligence has always been important to the armed forces, but efforts became even more vital during operations in Iraq and Afghanistan. During these missions, intelligence specialists gathered information from people living in villages who had contact with enemy soldiers or commanders. By talking to these villagers, Marine Corps intelligence specialists not only learned about enemy officers' plans, but also how these forces thought and behaved.

Intelligence specialists work in a variety of different situations. Many intelligence specialists work in the United States. These specialists may identify ways in which bases and air stations are at risk from enemy attacks. Specialists gather and analyze information that could aid an enemy and work to devise ways to keep that information more secure. Their responsibilities include researching, recording, and reporting on the information they gather.

Specialists in the United States and on bases in allied countries also gather intelligence on enemy countries and analyze it to understand what an adversary may be planning. These efforts are vital in protecting Marines in the field as well as soldiers and civilians at home in the United States.

Other intelligence specialists work in the field, deploying with a combat unit to make contact with people living in areas where Marines are fighting. Intelligence specialists in the field may spend much of their time building relationships with local residents, village elders, or officials from the government. This may include becoming familiar with foreign customs and learning the local language or dialect. Developing open communication with these people helps intelligence specialists gather information that is then passed along to Marine commanders to help them plan their attacks or improve safety in the field. Specialists may also speak with friendly, local leaders or captured enemy prisoners to gather information and evidence about enemy troop strength, movements, or intentions.

Soldiers often have little idea about what goes into finding the enemy or planning attacks, but it is the work of intelligence specialists that creates these plans. Even on a peacekeeping mission or a mission that does not involve direct combat, intelligence information is used to plan maneuvers so that Marines can complete their duties as quickly and efficiently as possible.

Intelligence specialists also work to protect troops in the field. As Moyer explains, "Any time we have Marines forward-deployed, there are other nations that want to collect information. Part of the effort is to identify what that foreign collection threat is and then inform Marines about it so that they hopefully do not divulge information that may be useful to an adversary."

How Do You Become an Intelligence Specialist?

Education

A high school diploma or the equivalent is required to enter the Marine Corps. High school students who have an interest in working as intelligence specialists should take courses in computers, communications, and foreign languages. Classes such as public speaking and psychology can also be useful for this career path.

After joining up and completing sixteen weeks of basic training with all other Marines, those interested in becoming intelligence specialists spend about four months at the Navy and Marine Corps Intelligence Training Center in Dam Neck, Virginia. Here they learn intelligence-gathering techniques and procedures as well as how the intelligence field supports the Marine Corps. Courses include intelligence preparation for the battlefield, orders of battle, map reading, report writing, briefing and debriefing, and much more.

Classes are extremely challenging. One Marine who completed the course was quoted in Harkins's article as saying, "The majority of the school is not academic, it's performance-based. You're put into scenarios and dealing with role players playing different types of people in those scenarios. There's often a lot of ambiguity when you're dealing with personalities and the way people think and act. It's not a science." This means that it takes a special skill or type of personality to succeed as an intelligence specialist. Personal qualities such as intuition are more important than doing well in a classroom exercise or on a written test.

Some Marines choose to go into intelligence from the start. Others move into the field from other assignments. An intelligence specialist will succeed based on his or her personality and skills rather than the specific Marine training that was received.

Certification and Licensing

No special certification or licensing is required. However, a Marine who is interested in becoming an intelligence specialist must be a US citizen and undergo a high-level security clearance and a background check. The Marine's family will also have to undergo a thorough background check.

Volunteer Work and Internships

Before entering the Marine Corps, students may benefit from finding volunteer work or internships working with people. Students can look for opportunities at local organizations that deal with the public. Work that involves speaking a foreign language can also benefit a prospective intelligence specialist.

Skills and Personality

An intelligence specialist must have good people skills. He or she must be able to form relationships with others and earn their trust. An intelligence specialist working in the field might be expected to make contacts with members of the enemy and earn their trust enough for them to reveal information. Intelligence specialists working on base usually work in teams, so they must also be good at working with other people.

Good communication is another essential skill for this career. Intelligence specialists must write reports and communicate verbally with other members of the team as well as with superior officers. Specialists may be asked to lead meetings and interact with other team members to gather information and plan strategies. As the specialist in a Military.com forum said, "This job requires a lot of time for research writing, studying, and thinking. . . . If you can't read/write coherently, now is a great time to practice because you will need to do it."

Intelligence specialists should also be analytical and have good problem-solving skills. They may be asked to analyze the data they gather and offer their interpretations about what the data mean. Specialists may be faced with questions about the information they study and need to figure out how to solve any problems it creates. Specialists working in the field also need to solve problems that may arise because of the intelligence information they receive, or they may need to figure out better ways to communicate with local residents so that they can obtain necessary information.

Patience is also a key trait. Gathering and analyzing data can take a long time. In the field, gaining the trust of informers and building relationships with local officials can often take time and cannot be rushed. Intelligence specialists must take time to analyze all information received in order to make the best conclusions, knowing that the answers or interpretations they provide may save lives.

On the Job

Working Conditions

Intelligence specialists may work in offices on base. They work with computers to gather and analyze data, and they spend time writing up reports on what useful information they have found. They often work in teams to share what they have learned and benefit from what others have discovered.

Other specialists may be deployed on missions in foreign countries. These specialists will usually live with the troops but spend much of their time in villages and other local gathering places to interact with informants. While in the field, specialists will have to face the same conditions as their fellow Marines, including harsh weather and climate, sleeping in the open, and enduring combat conditions.

Intelligence specialists who are deployed in the field often work twelve-hour days. They may work longer hours depending on the mission. Specialists who are not deployed usually have a more normal work schedule.

Earnings

As of June 2015, the average salary for an intelligence specialist in the Marine Corps was $51,646 per year. Intelligence specialists in the military also receive other benefits such as health insurance for themselves and their family and paid leave and time off. Marines also receive free housing on base or a housing allowance if they live off base.

Opportunities for Advancement

As with the other armed services, advancement in the Marines depends on an individual's performance and time served. As individuals gain more experience, they may go up in rank and receive greater opportunities. Marines who reach officer status have more opportunities than Marines who have a lower rank. Officers are often placed in supervisory positions and lead teams of intelligence specialists both in the United States and abroad.

To be considered for a counterintelligence job, a Marine must have at least the rank of corporal or sergeant. Some lance corporals are also considered. They must also be at least twenty-one years old and have at least three years left in the service once they complete the four-month intelligence school.

What Is the Future Outlook for Intelligence Specialists?

The future outlook for intelligence specialists is excellent. There is a constant demand for specialists, and those with the proper background and training are much in demand. Since 2014 the Marines have escalated their recruiting efforts for intelligence specialists, making this one of the most in-demand career opportunities in the corps.

What Are Employment Prospects in the Civilian World?

Intelligence specialists have many job opportunities in the civilian world. They often go on to work for the US government as intelligence analysts. Others work for independent military contractors. Many use their skills to go into a career as private investigators. In addition, the analytical and social skills possessed by intelligence specialists, as well as their excellent relationship and communication skills, make them highly qualified to work in many different industries in the civilian world.

Linguist

It would be unrealistic for every Marine to be trained to speak foreign languages fluently. That is where the job of a linguist comes into play. A Marine Corps linguist translates and interprets foreign languages. He or she is the point of communication—on the ground—for interacting with foreign civilians, soldiers, or prisoners. Marines train and employ linguists who speak almost every language on earth.

At a Glance:

Linguist

Minimum Educational Requirements
High school diploma or the equivalent

Personal Qualities
A good communicator, patient, detail oriented

Certification and Licensing
Defense Language Proficiency Test and security clearance

Working Conditions
In an office on base or in the field

Salary Range
Monthly salary depends on pay grade and years of service

Future Job Outlook
Above average growth rate through 2022

Linguists use their language skills in many different ways. They are responsible for language translation and interpretation activities to support all military operational and intelligence matters encountered during field operations and exercises. It is the linguist's responsibility to speak, read, and write one or more foreign languages and use these skills to help Marines communicate with the foreign individuals they encounter.

Linguists are especially important in intelligence work. A linguist may work with intelligence specialists to translate communications in foreign languages and help intelligence specialists understand what is being said or written. Linguists

39

are often part of intelligence teams who work to figure out what other countries or enemy forces are planning. One type of linguist, a cryptologic linguist, works to decode transmissions in other languages or in code that have been intercepted by intelligence sources. These linguists monitor, transcribe, and translate intercepted target communications, analyze foreign radio communications, and install, operate, and perform preventive maintenance on radio intercept equipment.

Linguists may be stationed in the United States or on bases around the world. These linguists generally work in an office setting. They listen to and read news broadcasts and translate information for other Marines to use. They may spend a great deal of time working on computers or listening to transmissions on headsets.

Sergeant Miguel Iles, who was named the US Department of Defense's Language Professional of the Year in 2013, learned Korean at a Marine Corps school and deployed to South Korea as part of a radio battalion. Iles served as a translator during joint military exercises between the United States and South Korea and also worked to process intelligence reports. Iles uses his knowledge of Korean and Chinese to understand the cultural background of these two countries. "I can read not only what the Western media is saying, but read the original press releases from North and South Korea, as well as commentary made by China," he said in an article titled "Marine Linguist Named Best in DoD" on the official Marine Corps website. "I find the Western media is very lazy when it comes to reporting from foreign media."

Other linguists may be deployed to combat missions. The linguist's skills are vital in ensuring the Marines know what is going on and can plan future actions. Linguists serve as translators and interpreters of the local language so that their Marine comrades can communicate with local residents as well as enemy soldiers. A linguist in the field may work translating documents or media reports. He or she may work with intelligence officers to understand intercepted messages and transmissions. A linguist might also serve as an interpreter for conversations with local residents or during questioning of prisoners of war. Sometimes they work with linguists from the armed forces of other countries. For example, the US Marines have worked with members of the Afghan National Army to translate and interpret the local language.

Linguists who work in the field face special challenges. Along with translating written or spoken words, they must also be careful to present the intent of those words accurately. The Marines state that a linguist's job is to interpret and translate foreign languages into English using phrasing that preserves the original intent and meaning of the words. In addition, linguists must avoid language that is stilted, unnatural, or difficult to understand and display an impartial attitude toward each speaker. Linguists may even be asked to interview non-English-speaking civilians and include their own opinion of the credibility of the person when writing up a report of the conversation.

Marine linguists have even found ways to help local residents who want to improve their lives. In an article titled "Face of Defense: Marine Linguists Aid Afghan Youth," published on the US Department of Defense website, Corporal Meredith Brown describes the work of Lance Corporals Lauren Kohls and Sarah Lowe. These two Pashto linguists teamed up to create a charity for Afghan youth called Hayla International. Hayla's goal is to provide resources to teach Afghan children how to read and write in their native language. "After being out here a while, we really saw the need for education," Lowe says. "We've seen kind of where this country is headed in the past however many years of war with no education, and people just not having futures and not have a chance to do something better for themselves." The two women see education as crucial to Afghan progress—and their language skills and understanding of Afghan culture made this project possible.

How Do You Become a Linguist?

Education

A high school diploma or the equivalent is required to enter the Marine Corps. High school students who have an interest in working as linguists should take as many foreign language courses as they can. Once a student has joined the Marines, he or she will take the Armed Services Vocational Aptitude Battery. In addition, anyone hoping for a career as a linguist must pass the Defense Language Aptitude Battery, which tests their ability to learn a foreign language.

After joining the Marine Corps and completing sixteen weeks of basic training, linguists attend the Defense Language Institute in Monterey, California, to learn a foreign language. Language school lasts for forty to eighty weeks, depending on the language chosen. The classes at the Defense Language Institute have been described as very intense. Students spend up to eight hours a day, five days a week, in the classroom, learning languages from native speakers in a complete immersion (only the foreign language is spoken) program, and these students must also attend study halls at night.

Even though the program is difficult and has a high failure rate, those who graduate say it is an amazing way to learn. As Iles said on the official Marine Corps website, "the program at the Defense Language Institute is great. I went from knowing just kimchi and hello in Korean to being able to understand newspaper articles and television news." After graduating from the Defense Language Institute, students planning to become cryptologic linguists are sent to an air force base in Texas for radio training and are then assigned to one of the radio battalions.

Certification and Licensing

No special certification or licensing is required. However, linguists must obtain and maintain a minimum proficiency level in listening, reading, or speaking on the Defense Language Proficiency Test, which is the current US Department of Defense standard for testing proficiency in a specific foreign language. Linguists who perform intelligence work must have top secret clearance, since their work is classified because of national security.

Volunteer Work and Internships

Before entering the Marine Corps, students may benefit from finding volunteer work or internships that allow them to use a foreign language, such as work in a foreign language–speaking community.

Skills and Personality

A linguist should have excellent foreign language skills. He or she should have an aptitude for learning foreign languages and find it easy to master new languages. Linguists should also be able to read and understand media reports in various formats, since they may be expected to use these accounts as part of their work with the Marines.

It is also important for linguists to be detail oriented. Paying close attention to how people communicate is vital in interpreting what they say and what they mean. Linguists should also have strong communication skills. They will often work as part of a team, especially in intelligence work, and will be expected to write reports or speak in front of a group to pass along information. Linguists may be asked to spend time on computers, so excellent computer and technical skills are also important.

Because a linguist's main responsibility is to communicate, he or she should be good at speaking and listening to other people. Linguists should also have good people skills, since much of their job involves speaking with others. It is also important for linguists to be able to understand subtext, or what people really mean by their words.

On the Job

Working Conditions

A linguist may work in several different environments. Some linguists work in an office. They may spend the day reading and writing reports, working on a computer, or attending meetings. Cryptologic linguists may spend most of their day sitting in a room listening to intercepted transmissions through a headset and transcribing what they hear into English for use by intelligence specialists. A linguist working on base can expect to work regular hours during the week and have weekends off, although he or she may have to work longer hours during certain missions.

A linguist may also be deployed as part of a military campaign. Linguists in the field may face harsh conditions in terms of weather, climate, and housing facilities. They may have to work long hours under dangerous conditions, communicating with native residents or transcribing transmissions or documents into English.

Earnings

As of June 2015, the average salary for a linguist in the Marine Corps was $42,121 per year. People who enter the military with the ability to speak a foreign language qualify for extra monthly pay. Linguists in the military also receive other benefits such as health insurance for themselves and their family and paid leave and time off. Marines also receive free housing on base or a housing allowance if they live off base.

Opportunities for Advancement

As with the other armed services, advancement in the Marines depends on an individual's performance and time served. As individuals gain more experience, they may go up in rank and receive greater opportunities.

Linguists are in great demand in the Marines. A Marine who has a facility for languages can advance into jobs with more responsibilities. He or she may become a supervisor or a leader of a team working on linguistic or intelligence projects. Marines may also advance by learning additional languages.

What Is the Future Outlook for Linguists?

The future outlook for linguists is positive. Since the Marines deploy around the world and work with many other countries, they are always looking for recruits who can speak foreign languages.

What Are Employment Prospects in the Civilian World?

Linguists have many job opportunities in the civilian world. Their ability to speak foreign languages makes linguists valuable hires in both government and civilian occupations. Many international companies need employees who speak other languages in order to compete in the global market. In addition to job opportunities in the United States, a linguist with experience in other languages and cultures may also be able to find work in foreign countries.

Mechanic

What Does a Mechanic Do?

The Marine Corps is a combined arms force that includes coverage of air, land, and sea. As with any branch of the armed forces, the Marines rely on transportation equipment to get them where they need to go. To achieve this goal, the Marines operate one of the largest aviation fleets in the world and also utilize tens of thousands of trucks, tanks, rescue vehicles, and repair vehicles. All of these vehicles need to be in good running order to operate when needed. For this reason, mechanics are a vital part of the corps.

Mechanics in the Marine Corps work on aircraft or vehicles such as trucks and tanks. Others work on specialty vehicles like amphibious assault vehicles that can operate on land or sea. Mechanics are responsible for maintaining and repairing all vehicles in the fleet. Marine mechanics install, remove, inspect, test, maintain, and repair all systems on vehicles used on land, in the sea, or in the air. They work on all parts of these vehicles, including mechanical and electrical components. Mechanics may replace parts, including engines,

At a Glance:

Mechanic

Minimum Educational Requirements
High school diploma or the equivalent

Personal Qualities
Patient, detail oriented, mechanically minded, good problem solver

Certification and Licensing
For aircraft mechanics, FAA airframe and powerplant license; for auto mechanics, ASE certifications

Working Conditions
In garages, airplane hangars, or repair stations

Salary Range
Monthly salary depends on pay grade and years of service

Number of Jobs
As of 2013 about 21,806

Future Job Outlook
Average growth rate through 2022

windows, doors, and other parts of the vehicle. Whereas some parts of a vehicle may be easy to replace and repair, others may be more difficult to reach. Since many vehicles used in wartime are heavily armored for protection, a mechanic might have to remove hundreds of pounds of armor to get at a component in need of repair.

Mechanics have a wide variety of responsibilities. They perform checks and maintenance on a constant basis to make sure vehicles are ready to use. They also inspect vehicles and perform repairs following each mission. Mechanics are responsible for maintaining equipment, troubleshooting or solving problems, repairing or replacing faulty equipment, rewiring or replacing electrical circuits, upgrading equipment, and testing equipment to make sure it is working properly.

The Marines could not function without experienced mechanics to maintain and repair their vehicles. In an article titled "Marine Mechanics Ensure Success During Combat Operations in Afghanistan" on the US Marine Corps website, the author, Corporal Joseph Scanlan, describes the work of a battalion of Marines stationed in Helmand Province, Afghanistan, in 2014. Scanlan writes:

> From sunrise until sunset, the clicks of ratchets and whines of power drills can be heard every day as the mechanics of 1st Battalion, 7th Marine Regiment, continuously work on vehicles to ensure mission success. Finishing each day covered in motor oil, transmission fluid, dirt, and sweat, five lance corporal mechanics are the only individuals responsible for all vehicle maintenance.

Gunnery Sergeant Michael Shuman, the motor transportation chief of the battalion, adds, "There is a lot of responsibility that rests on their shoulders. They have a work ethic that I can't even describe; it's just phenomenal. They continue to push nonstop."

Mechanics are especially vital in battalions stationed in war zones. Without the guarantee of vehicles that are in good shape and ready to roll, the lives of the Marines would be in great danger. It is up to the motor transportation mechanics to make sure each vehicle is functioning properly. Vehicles must be ready for use at all times, and any repairs must be made quickly and without delay.

It is also important for mechanics to be ready to fix a vehicle wherever and whenever it breaks down and to work as long as necessary to fix a problem. Repairs on the road can range from simple flat tires to complete engine failure. Overheating is a common problem, along with the wear and tear that rough terrain puts on the engines.

In his article "Motor Transport Mechanics Keep 22nd MEU's Vehicles Rolling" on the official Marine Corps website, Sergeant Matt C. Preston describes the work of motor pool mechanics serving in Afghanistan in 2004. He explains that repairing vehicles quickly is a matter of survival for soldiers driving through enemy territory. Convoys that are not moving are easy targets for attack. "We've got to do a quick fix, whatever keeps them rolling," says Corporal Jeremy Leopold, a motor transport mechanic with MEU Service Support Group 22, who was interviewed by Preston for his article. Making repairs quickly is critical. "You never know when you're going to be ambushed. You try to keep it to a fifteen-minute time limit."

Mechanics spend most of their time doing general maintenance and repair tasks. Parts such as filters and fuel pumps are constantly being replaced. Vehicles also face a lot of damage from rough roads and mines or other explosive devices. According to Scanlan's article, Marine mechanics in Helmand Province spend a lot of time replacing bulletproof windows on their vehicles. These specially made windows are constantly being damaged by gunfire, shrapnel, and rocks. They can weigh up to 400 pounds (181 kg) and take hours to replace.

"Sometimes I have to sit in the sun all day when I'm trying to get a vehicle to work," Lance Corporal Andrew Witte said in Scanlan's article. "Sometimes things just don't go my way and it takes a lot longer than it should to fix a problem, but it's one of the greatest feelings when I get a vehicle fixed. I love being a mechanic because it's a very rewarding MOS [military occupational specialty]."

How Do You Become a Mechanic?

Education

A high school diploma or the equivalent is required to enter the Marine Corps. High school students who have an interest in working as a mechanic should take vocational courses in vehicle repair.

After joining the Marine Corps and completing sixteen weeks of basic training, or boot camp, mechanics train at one of several schools to learn how to repair and maintain a variety of Marine vehicles. Courses include classroom instruction as well as hands-on training on a variety of different vehicles and their parts.

Certification and Licensing

In addition to the courses required by the Marines, the FAA requires all aircraft mechanics to be certified by taking courses approved by the FAA, including the licensing course for airframe and powerplant. Vehicle mechanics may obtain Automotive Service Excellence (ASE) certifications by taking courses and showing relevant work experience.

Volunteer Work and Internships

Before entering the Marine Corps, students may benefit from finding volunteer work or internships in auto or aircraft repair and maintenance. Students may look for opportunities at local auto repair shops or technical schools.

Skills and Personality

A mechanic must be detail oriented and good at identifying and solving problems. He or she should be able to troubleshoot easily and to identify problems and figure out their solutions quickly and competently. Critical-thinking skills are important in this field, as well as being a good listener in order to gather clues and identify what is causing the problem. A mechanic must also be able to work under pressure and as part of a team. Communication with other team members is an essential part of the job since mechanics must work together to diagnose and repair issues.

Because many vehicles have sophisticated electrical and computer systems, a mechanic should have strong computer skills. He or she should also be interested in electronics. In addition, mechanics must keep detailed and accurate records of all equipment inspections, repairs, and maintenance work, so attention to detail and the ability to organize and keep good notes are very important.

Mechanics work with a variety of different tools. They should have strong mechanical skills and good eye-hand coordination. They may work under a great deal of pressure. They must meet tight deadlines and stay on schedule without rushing through their work or cutting corners. This is especially true for mechanics working in a war zone. It is essential that mechanics be thorough, meticulous, and careful to make sure that the vehicles they are working on are safe and can be relied on to perform.

On the Job

Working Conditions

Mechanics work in several different environments. Some mechanics may work in a repair shop or a garage. Others may work outside to repair vehicles in the field. Mechanics must be able to stand for long periods of time and be able to crouch down to fit into tight spaces. Some of their work may involve physical strength, such as lifting heavy parts. Repair work is often messy because of the vehicle's oil, grease, and other fluids.

Mechanics who are stationed with a combat battalion get very little time off. Although many Marines are able to catch up on rest after a mission, mechanics working in a war zone may have long hours of work waiting for them as soon as they return from a mission. Mechanics must perform preventive and regularly scheduled maintenance, fix broken parts, and ensure that every vehicle is ready to go for the very next mission as soon as possible. For this reason, there are no days off for mechanics in a war zone.

Earnings

As of June 2015, the average salary for a mechanic in the Marine Corps was $38,000 per year. Mechanics in the military also receive other benefits such as health insurance for themselves and their family and paid leave and time off. Marines also receive free housing on base or a housing allowance if they live off base.

Opportunities for Advancement

As with the other armed services, advancement in the Marines depends on an individual's performance and time served. As individuals gain more experience, they may go up in rank and receive greater opportunities.

It is important for mechanics to stay up-to-date in their field. Equipment is constantly being upgraded and improved, and mechanics must keep up with these changes. They may need to read technical articles and take refresher courses to stay current or advance in this field.

As a Marine mechanic is promoted, he or she will take on additional responsibility for repair and administrative requirements for multiple systems. An individual can advance to a supervisory position or choose to become an officer if he or she meets the educational and aptitude qualifications.

What Is the Future Outlook for Mechanics?

The Marine Corps operates one of the largest aviation and vehicle fleets in the world, so there is a great demand for mechanics. According to the Bureau of Labor Statistics, opportunities in the armed forces should remain good through the year 2022. The Marines, like other branches of the armed services, constantly need to fill both entry-level and professional positions as members are promoted through the ranks, leave the service, or retire.

What Are Employment Prospects in the Civilian World?

Mechanics have many job opportunities in the civilian world. Civilian mechanics are employed by car and truck repair shops, vehicle manufacturers, and vehicle fleet companies. The federal government and nongovernmental agencies may also provide employment opportunities. Knowing how to keep air, land, and sea vehicles in good working order is a valuable skill that can translate into a positive job outlook in the civilian world.

Military Police Officer

Like civilian police officers, military police keep law and order and make sure people are safe and obeying the laws. Unlike their civilian counterparts, military police officers can only enforce laws on military property and for military personnel. The military uses its own police force because military bases have their own rules and command structure, and military police are trained to handle special situations that may arise there. Being a military police officer in the Marines requires the ability to manage people and make sure they are following the rules.

Military police officers are employed at every major base and installation to protect people and property and enforce military law. Their duties may include basic jobs such as manning gates and security checkpoints and enforcing traffic laws and military regulations on base. Their duties may also include investigating crimes and terrorist acts. Military police officers are responsible for keeping order on military bases and guarding points of entrance. They may arrest soldiers

At a Glance:
Military Police Officer

Minimum Educational Requirements
High school diploma or the equivalent

Personal Qualities
Confident, thorough, able to work in a team, good people skills

Working Conditions
Indoors or outside, standing guard or on patrol

Salary Range
Monthly salary depends on pay grade and years of service

Future Job Outlook
Average growth rate through 2022

A Marine Corps police officer checks the bag of an Iraqi civilian who has been detained. Military police may work in combat zones or on military bases, where they deal with crimes involving US military personnel.

who break the law while on these bases. These officers may also become involved if a service member breaks a law while off base.

A military police officer has many responsibilities, but these can be summed up as five main functions: maintain order and law; perform police intelligence operations; maintain area security posts and security operations; act as resettlement and internment officers in various internment operations (for example, helping refugees or prisoners settle into resettlement centers or prisons); and act as support for mobility operations (directing traffic or otherwise assisting in the movement of troops and munitions). Military police officers perform assigned law enforcement duties to uphold the law, maintain order and discipline, and support the commander's law enforcement and security requirements in both peacetime and combat operations.

Military police officers may patrol in vehicles or on foot, securing areas or finding lawbreakers. Some work with specially trained military police dogs. These officers and their dogs may conduct vehicle searches and search open areas, buildings, or vehicles for explosives or illegal drugs. Military police officers and their dogs may also search for people who are lost or wanted by the law.

Military police officers who serve in combat zones have a different set of responsibilities. Along with protecting lives and property, they may also work as the security team for motor convoys through hostile territory, act as security for senior officers or visiting dignitaries, or serve in other ways to protect troops in hostile territory. They may also train and coordinate with local police and security. Military police officers in combat zones may also handle prisoners and secure and process detainees before sending them to military holding facilities or prisons.

Military police officers have taken on increased responsibility for maintaining law and order in war-torn areas such as Iraq and Afghanistan. During the recent wars in those countries, military police officers have taken on the roles of training local residents to serve as police and maintain law and order after the US forces leave. Military police officers also gather intelligence, secure evidence, and assist local authorities to make arrests to take down criminal networks. After a building or other site is raided for enemy activity, military police officers may come in to investigate the site for clues to help them track down insurgents and terrorists.

In a 2012 article in the *Marine Corps Times*, author Julie Watson described how the Marine Corps had created three special military police battalions that can quickly deploy around the world to help investigate crimes from terrorism to drug trafficking, and train new security forces. Each battalion is made up of roughly five hundred military police officers and dozens of dogs. In the past, Marine Corps military police focused mostly on providing security to convoys or guarding generals and other dignitaries on visits to dangerous regions. By creating the new battalions, the corps hoped to use police officers' investigative skills and training to solve major crimes around the world. "Over the past 11 years of combat operations in Iraq and Afghanistan, some lessons learned painfully, there has been a growing appreciation and a demand for, on the part of the war fighter, the unique skills and capabilities that MPs [military police] bring to the fight," Major Jan Durham, commander of the First Law Enforcement Battalion at Camp Pendleton, says in Watson's article. "We do enforce traffic laws and we do write reports and tickets, and that's good, but we do so much more than that."

How Do You Become a Military Police Officer?

Education

A high school diploma or the equivalent is required to enter the Marine Corps. High school students who have an interest in working as military police should take courses in criminal justice.

After joining the Marine Corps and completing sixteen weeks of basic training, a Marine interested in becoming a military police officer will be sent to Fort Leonard Wood in Missouri, which is a US Army Military Police School. Marine Corps military police take a three-month Basic Military Police Course at Fort Leonard Wood. Military police officers who are chosen to work as dog handlers will also take the Military Working Dog Basic Handler Course and the Detector Dog Handler Course at Lackland Air Force Base in San Antonio, Texas.

Volunteer Work and Internships

Before entering the Marine Corps, students may benefit from finding volunteer work or internships in the criminal justice or security fields. Students can look for opportunities with local organizations, police benevolent leagues, or companies looking for security guards or assistance with crowd control.

Skills and Personality

A military police officer should have a strong presence and leadership abilities. He or she must be firm in enforcing the law and able to convince people to obey without any trouble. It is important for a police officer to be good at identifying and solving problems before events get out of hand. He or she must be able to work under pressure and as part of a team.

Critical-thinking skills are important in this field, as well as being a good listener in order to gather clues and identify what is causing the problem. A military police officer should have good communications skills. It is also important for a police officer to be patient and not jump to conclusions. Officers must be able to handle tense, often dangerous, situations calmly and rationally.

Military police officers should have a clear understanding of the law and what they can and cannot do. They should also be good at keeping records, since they may be asked to write down the details of their patrols or other responsibilities.

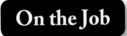

On the Job

Working Conditions

Military police officers are responsible for policing the armed forces and preventing criminal activity by military or civilian personnel. They enforce the law on military bases in the United States and other parts of the world. Because they are members of the armed forces, military police officers are generally not allowed to work on civilian law enforcement or serve as police outside of a military base. There are exceptions, however. Military police officers may perform traffic control and traffic stops on federal property. They may also serve off base if martial law has been declared.

Although some parts of a military police officer's job are routine, such as manning security posts or enforcing traffic laws, this job can also be very dangerous. Military police officers may be asked to confront dangerous people or be faced with violence at a moment's notice.

Military police officers may work indoors or outdoors. They may work in a security booth or at a checkpoint, or they may be asked to patrol a building or an area on foot or in a vehicle. Police officers should have good physical stamina and be able to work long hours under tense conditions.

Officers who are deployed on combat missions may face difficult living conditions as well as danger from combat or terrorist activities. They must have strong survival skills and be able to work well with a team to keep themselves and other members of their battalion safe and secure.

Military police officers may also be deployed into the community when serving in war zones. They may interact with local residents and help resolve disputes between them and soldiers or assist local officials in combating crime.

Earnings

As of June 2015, salaries for military police officers in the Marine Corps range from $36,433 to $39,462, with an average salary of $37,947 per year. Military police officers also receive other benefits such as health insurance for themselves and their family and paid leave and time off. Marines also receive free housing on base or a housing allowance if they live off base.

Opportunities for Advancement

As with the other armed services, advancement in the Marines depends on an individual's performance and time served. As individuals gain more experience, they may go up in rank and receive greater opportunities.

The website USMilitary.com reports that "Marine Corps 2nd Lieutenants that start their career in the Military Police have nearly unlimited room for advancement, and they lead from the front. Working in the Military Police gives a 2nd Lieutenant seasoning and experience that can act well in dealing with other experiences down the road in their career."

As a Marine military police officer is promoted, he or she can rise in rank until he or she becomes a military police captain. A military police captain is responsible for two hundred to three hundred soldiers, as well as assisting with police and military police operations at the battalion and command level.

What Is the Future Outlook for Military Police Officers?

The Marine Corps maintains a strong military police force, so opportunities in this field should remain steady. According to the Bureau of Labor Statistics, opportunities in the armed forces should remain good through the year 2022. The Marines, like other branches of the armed services, constantly need to fill both entry-level and professional positions as members are promoted through the ranks, leave the service, or retire.

What Are Employment Prospects in the Civilian World?

Military police officers can find many job opportunities in the civilian world. Because of their training, they can qualify for jobs in civilian police forces. Some major city police forces will provide extra pay or waive education requirements for candidates who have experience as military police officers. In addition, many police departments, both large and small, work with police dogs, so a military police officer with dog handler training can find good employment opportunities in this field as well.

Some military police officers go on to careers with the US Secret Service, which protects the president and other important members of the government. The Secret Service actively recruits officers from the military and gives veterans special consideration. It also welcomes candidates who have experience in law enforcement or investigation. Similarly, the FBI also gives special consideration to veterans with military police experience.

Small Arms Technician

What Does a Small Arms Technician Do?

The Marine Corps states that "every Marine is a rifleman." This means that all Marines are, first and foremost, soldiers who receive intense combat training. Even if a Marine is a cook or a supply clerk, he or she will know how to use a weapon. Therefore, the weapons used by the Marines must be repaired and maintained in good working order.

Although the riflemen, or Marines who actually use the guns in combat or exercises, have the primary responsibility for keeping their weapons in good condition, they are not the only ones who make sure handheld weapons function properly. Small arms technicians are also a vital part of making sure Marine weapons are ready to use.

Small arms include rifles, pistols, machine guns, and any other weapon that can be carried by hand. A small arms technician is responsible for fixing most of the small arms that are in use by Marine Corps units. It is the technician's responsibility to make sure that the weapons needed to perform the mission are in good working order.

Small arms technicians op-

At a Glance:
Small Arms Technician

Minimum Educational Requirements
High school diploma or the equivalent

Personal Qualities
Detail oriented, logical, good eye-hand coordination

Working Conditions
Inside an armory

Salary Range
Monthly salary depends on pay grade and years of service

Future Job Outlook
Average growth rate through 2022

erate under the supervision of more senior enlisted personnel. Small arms technicians perform basic duties that keep a unit's weapons in top condition, including inspection, repair, and cleaning. They provide additional services beyond what riflemen do to take care of their weapons.

Small arms technicians have other responsibilities besides maintaining weapons. An important part of the job is to keep administrative records, maintenance and repair forms, and technical manuals. They even inventory other carried equipment—such as radios, night-vision technology, and navigation devices—that are commonly stored in an armory. A technician may also be responsible for organizing personnel, scheduling preventive maintenance, maintaining proper ordnance (military weapons and equipment) procedures, testing ordnance, conducting inspections, and training others, especially as he or she rises in rank and experience.

How Do You Become a Small Arms Technician?

Education

A high school diploma or the equivalent is required to enter the Marine Corps. High school students who have an interest in working as small arms technicians should take courses in math and physics. Experience using firearms would also be valuable. Once a student has joined the Marines, he or she will take the Armed Services Vocational Aptitude Battery, or ASVAB. To qualify as a small arms repair candidate, a soldier must have a raw score of 95 or higher on the Mechanical Maintenance part of the ASVAB.

Candidates for small arms technician jobs must also pass the Command Arms Ammunition and Explosives screening. They are not allowed to have any convictions in their military or civilian career involving drugs, theft, or larceny.

After joining the Marine Corps and completing sixteen weeks of basic training, or boot camp, a small arms technician must complete the Marine Small Arms Repair Course. This course is offered at Fort

Lee in Virginia and takes about three months. Training focuses on understanding basic ordnance, construction, administration, and small gun handling; how to inspect guns, rifles, small arms, and other weaponry; and how to analyze and repair a weapon so that it returns to its original condition or better. Students also learn repair and armory operational procedures.

Small arms technicians may also attend a Marine Combat Training (MCT) course. This course provides combat skills training to non-infantry Marines to assure that "every Marine is a rifleman." Training includes marksmanship, combat formations and patrolling, and other combat-related skills. One Marine who attended both the training course and infantry school described the experience on Yahoo! Answers this way: "MCT is a watered down version of infantry school. I was one of the fortunate few who had to attend both schools. You do a lot of tactical training, but nothing too advanced. You will learn how to patrol, set up ambushes, and establish a defensive position. You will go on some hikes. I believe the longest is fifteen miles."

Skills and Personality

A small arms technician must be detail oriented and good at identifying and solving problems. Small arms technicians should be able to troubleshoot easily and to identify problems and figure out their solutions quickly and competently. Critical-thinking skills are important in this field, as well as being a good listener in order to gather clues and identify what is causing the problem.

A small arms technician must also be good at mechanical tasks. He or she will need to put expensive equipment together quickly, competently, and safely. He or she must be able to work under pressure and as part of a team. Communication with other team members is an essential part of the job.

Because they are responsible for maintaining and repairing weapons, these technicians should be able to quickly identify how every weapon is put together and what parts make up each weapon. Accuracy is very important when repairing weapons, and a successful small arms technician must be able to perform the job quickly and efficiently without making mistakes.

Small arms technicians may also be asked to test equipment to make sure it is working properly. They must understand the requirements for proper operation of a weapon and make sure test results are accurate and reliable.

In addition to their repairing and maintenance tasks, small arms technicians must also keep accurate records of their work. They will need to list the inspections and repairs they have made and describe how they corrected a problem. These records help maintain safety standards and keep track of any problems.

On the Job

Working Conditions

Small arms technicians can expect to spend the vast majority of their time in the armory, which is the place guns are stored and repaired. A typical day might include rising at 5:30 a.m. and attending a physical training session. After breakfast, each soldier is expected at a company formation about seven o'clock. After formation, a technician will likely spend the better part of the day doing weapons maintenance in the armory.

Although riflemen are responsible for cleaning their weapons after they are used, small arms technicians are the ones who perform what is called "second echelon maintenance." This type of maintenance includes taking weapons apart to repair or service them. Technicians may also inspect weapons for cleanliness when they are returned at the end of the day.

Small arms technicians are likely to be assigned to an infantry group and are also likely to be deployed. Repair technicians are a vital part of any infantry unit in a combat zone because weapons must be inspected, repaired, and kept in good working order at all times.

Other small arms technicians may be stationed at a base in the United States or an allied country. In her article, "Armorers Maintain Weapons, Ensure Marine Corps Readiness," published on the Defense Video & Imagery Distribution System website, Lance Corporal Elizabeth Case talks to several small arms technicians at a Marine Corps armory in Okinawa, Japan. According to Case, the day starts at 2:30 a.m., when the technicians begin issuing weapons for the day's operations and training. They make sure that all firearms are functional and in good condition.

Technicians are responsible for conducting a limited technical inspection as well as a prefire inspection before the weapons are used. In Case's article, Corporal Jason D. Dospoy, a small arms repairer and technician with Headquarters and Service Battalion, Marine Corps Base Camp Smedley D. Butler, Marine Corps Installations Pacific, explains, "We have (tools) that tell us if a weapon is serviceable or not. If something is wrong, we investigate the issue and if we cannot figure out the problem, we mark it with a yellow tag, signifying the weapon is down." Common problems include cracked or worn parts and obstructed gun barrels.

Corporal Shields L. Woods, a small arms technician with the Headquarters and Service Battalion, explains in Case's article why he finds his job so satisfying. "I like the maintenance," says Woods. "When we get a weapon that's broken and figure out what is wrong with it, it is like solving a mystery. There's a satisfaction that comes with accomplishing something like that."

Woods also believes that small arms technicians are vital to the Marine Corps' mission. "The Marine Corps' mission is to fight our nation's battles and win wars," he states. "We can't do that with the weapons systems if the systems are not properly maintained. We make sure they are always operational. Infantry Marines can't shoot without their weapons being at their best."

Earnings

As of June 2015, the average salary for a small arms technician in the Marine Corps was $37,894 per year. Small arms technicians in the military also receive other benefits such as health insurance for themselves and their family and paid leave and time off. Marines also receive free housing on base or a housing allowance if they live off base.

Opportunities for Advancement

As with the other armed services, advancement in the Marines depends on an individual's performance and time served. As individuals gain more experience, they may go up in rank and receive greater opportunities.

As a Marine small arms technician is promoted, he or she will take on additional responsibility for repair and administrative requirements. An individual can advance to a supervisory position or choose to become an officer if he or she meets the educational and aptitude qualifications. A small arms technician who has reached the level of corporal or higher may be responsible for training, supervising, and assisting in small arms inspection and repair. Supervisors may also be required to keep a maintenance schedule, assign shop duties, and assist in repairing small arms to specific standards.

What Is the Future Outlook for Small Arms Technicians?

According to the Bureau of Labor Statistics, opportunities in the armed forces should remain good through the year 2022. The Marines, like other branches of the armed services, constantly need to fill both entry-level and professional positions as members are promoted through the ranks, leave the service, or retire.

Since the Marine Corps cannot operate without weapons, there will always be a need for small arms technicians. Therefore, the outlook for these jobs should remain high.

What Are Employment Prospects in the Civilian World?

Although there is not as much use for small arms maintenance and repair in the civilian world, small arms technicians may be able to find employment at a weapons manufacturer, a weapons-based business, or a gun range. They may also find work at a government or private contractor working with weapons for combat situations.

However, many employers prize workers who have strong senses of discipline and responsibility, which are values that any Marine veteran should possess. Small arms technicians will likely be able to transfer their Marine training and values into various jobs in the civilian world, even if the jobs are not strictly related to weapons training and repair.

Tank Crewman

What Does a Tank Crewman Do?

The website USMilitary.com describes the job of a tank crewman, or tanker, as follows: "The enlisted person who seeks to join the Marine Corps that wants to be a M1 Tank crewman is a person who will have an adventurous and exciting job ahead of them." Tank crewmen have the responsibility of preparing, operating, maintaining, firing, and maneuvering the mighty tanks used by the Marine Corps. Crewmen are also responsible for checking and maintaining the ammunition, weapons, night-vision equipment, and other equipment carried on board the tanks.

These days the term *tank crewman* can refer to a man or a woman. Although women have been part of the Marines for many years, they were not allowed to serve as tank crewmen or in any other combat positions until 2012. In that year the Marines began assigning women to combat units, including tank battalions.

Tanks are an essential part of most military operations. Their size, power, and armor make them an excellent way to break through enemy defenses. Today's tanks are shielded with heavy armor and possess sophisticated electronic systems that allow tank crewmen to maneuver through all kinds of situations. Since the Marines is the branch of service that is most often first on the scene of battle

At a Glance:
Tank Crewman

Minimum Educational Requirements
High school diploma or the equivalent

Personal Qualities
Able to work in a team, able to remain calm under pressure, able to function in enclosed spaces

Working Conditions
Inside fighting vehicles

Salary Range
Monthly salary depends on pay grade and years of service

Future Job Outlook
Good

and therefore faces enemy forces head-on, tank crewmen have a vital job to perform. The Marines often rely on tanks' breaching power and destructive capacity to help get tough jobs done quickly.

There are several different types of tank crewmen. The tank gunner locates targets and operates the main weapon. The loader pulls shells from ammunition storage and loads them into the main gun. The tank driver moves the vehicle and positions it to fire on a target. The tank commander supervises maintenance and operation of the tank and makes decisions for the entire crew. In addition, all members of a tank crew work together to ensure their vehicle is in good repair and ready for operations.

The main battle tank of the Marines is the 70-ton (63.5-metric-ton) M1A1 Abrams. This is a heavily armored, well-armed tank with a powerful engine. The M1A1 can reach speeds of 45 miles per hour (72 kph) and hurl 120 mm shells 4,379 yards (4,000 m) with astounding accuracy. Each tank platoon includes four M1A1 Abrams. A tank platoon's job is chiefly to provide armor-protected firepower to support ground forces.

An M1A1 tank crew functions as a unit to operate the tank and its weapons. A list of an M1A1 crewman's duties may include preparing the tank; assembling equipment, personnel, and supplies for movement; preparing ammunition for firing; driving the tank; aiming, loading, and firing weapons; locating targets; and other various tank crew–type responsibilities.

After completing their training, most tank crewmen will be stationed with tank battalions either in Fort Lejeune in North Carolina or Twentynine Palms in California. Some tank crewmen are stationed on the Marine Corps base in Okinawa, Japan. Tank battalions deploy on a rotating schedule, so a tank crewman may be sent into a war zone at some point in his or her career.

How Do You Become a Tank Crewman?

Education

A high school diploma or the equivalent is required to enter the Marine Corps. High school students who have an interest in working as

Marine Corps tank crewmen prepare for an exercise involving tankers and infantry. Proper maintenance and operation of tanks, ammunition, and other related equipment are the responsibility of tank crewman.

tank crewmen should take courses in math and physics. Students may also wish to take a vocational course in mechanics or vehicle repair and maintenance.

After joining the Marine Corps and completing sixteen weeks of basic training, or boot camp, tank crewmen must complete the M1A1 Armor Crewman Course at Fort Knox in Kentucky. Here they will learn to drive the tank and operate its weapons, as well as learn how to maintain and repair it and all its weapons and equipment. This course includes both classroom training and training in simulated combat.

After completing the M1A1 Armor Crewman Course, candidates may then go on to attend another course at Fort Knox, called the M1A1 Reserve Tank Gunner/Commander Course. This is a nineteen-day advanced training course that targets the skills necessary to be a certified M1A1 crewman. After completing this course, the candidate will be given the opportunity to demonstrate his or her skills to the instructor/inspector of the battalion. After successfully demonstrating their skills, soldiers are certified as M1A1 tank crewmen.

Skills and Personality

Perhaps the most important skill necessary to become successful tank crewmen is good mechanical ability. They should be good at figuring out how things work. Crewmen should also be good at working with their hands and have good eye-hand coordination. Tank crewmen are required to use a variety of different tools to perform their job. They must be able to perform repairs and inspect and maintain equipment that costs millions of dollars.

Because tank crewmen often operate in dangerous situations in the field of battle, they should be able to remain calm under pressure. The inside of a tank is very small and closed in. For this reason, it is essential that tank crew members be able to work successfully in enclosed spaces. Because of their enclosed surroundings, they must not be claustrophobic or subject to panic attacks. They also need to be able to work quickly and focus on their jobs in spite of dangerous distractions.

The crew of a tank must be able to work successfully as a team. Tank crewmen work together to do their jobs, operate and maintain their vehicle, and provide protection for their fellow Marines. It is essential that crew members work well together under pressure and be able to communicate successfully even in difficult or dangerous situations.

On the Job

Working Conditions

After completing basic training in the United States, tank crewmen may be deployed into war zones or other unsettled areas around the world. They must be able to do their jobs under difficult situations, working in an enclosed area inside combat vehicles. Tank crewmen generally work in the field when they are deployed. Here they may face difficult and dangerous conditions, including attacks by enemy weapons. Victor Epand served as a tank crewman in the Marines for several years. He described the experience as physically difficult, but ultimately rewarding. In a post on Streetdirectory.com, Epand explained, "Being a Marine Corps tanker is the way to go. . . . If you want a great adventure, a way to be a part of a front line combat force without some of the more extreme hardships of the infantry, I definitely recommend Marine Corps tanks. Only join though if you can stand the very real possibility of getting sent into combat, killing and possibly dying." He went on to describe the daily hardships of a tank crewman's life:

> "Tanking" is challenging but very rewarding. . . . When it is cold, you are cold. When it is very cold you are very cold. When it rains, you are wet. Being wet and cold can last for days. Wet, cold, and deprived of sleep. Same when it's hot or when it's very hot. You get dirtier out in the field than you would believe. All of this stuff is awesome. . . . Like I said, I wouldn't trade that experience for the world.

Earnings

As of June 2015, the average salary for a tank crewman in the Marine Corps was $68,473 per year. Tank crewmen, like other members of the military, also receive other benefits such as health insurance for themselves and their family and paid leave and time off. Marines also receive free housing on base or a housing allowance if they live off base.

Opportunities for Advancement

As with the other armed services, advancement in the Marines depends on an individual's performance and time served. As individuals gain more experience, they may go up in rank and receive greater opportunities.

As a tank crewman is promoted, he or she will take on additional responsibility for supervising other crew members, making maintenance and repair decisions, and leading missions. An individual can advance to a supervisory position or choose to become an officer if he or she meets the educational and aptitude qualifications.

What Is the Future Outlook for Tank Crewmen?

The Marine Corps operates a large fleet of tanks, and these vehicles are an essential part of the Marine Corps weaponry. This means that there is a steady demand for tank crewmen. According to the Bureau of Labor Statistics, opportunities in the armed forces should remain good through the year 2022. The Marines, like other branches of the armed services, constantly need to fill both entry-level and professional positions as members are promoted through the ranks, leave the service, or retire.

What Are Employment Prospects in the Civilian World?

Although there is not a great demand for tank crewmen in the civilian world, these members of the armed forces may be able to find employment at a weapons manufacturer or a weapons-based business or at a gun range. They may also find work with a government or private contractor or be able to use their mechanical skills at a manufacturer of tanks and other armored vehicles.

However, many employers prize workers who have strong senses of discipline and responsibility, which are values that any Marine veteran should possess. Tank crewmen will likely be able to transfer their Marine training and values into various jobs in the civilian world, even if these jobs are not strictly related to operating an armored vehicle and using its weapons.

Interview with a Field Artillery Cannoneer

Corporal Michael Simpson is a field artillery cannoneer in the US Marine Corps. He is currently stationed at Camp Pendleton in California. Simpson answered questions about his career by e-mail.

Q: Why did you join the Marine Corps?

A: I joined the Marine Corps because of the history and traditions and the way I saw Marines hold themselves. I grew up always wanting to join the military—especially since 9/11—and thought it was the right time in my life after I finished at the local community college. The Marines are the toughest out of any branch and have hands down the hardest boot camp of any of the services, so I wanted that challenge of earning the title Marine. Basically I joined to give back to my country and to look back when I'm sixty and be content and say, "Yeah, I did my time."

Q: Why did you become a field artillery cannoneer? Did you choose this career, or did the Marines choose it for you?

A: I originally signed a combat support contract with the hopes of being a tanker, but it came down to the needs of the Marine Corps. You don't get to pick your exact job in the Marines since the motto is, "Every Marine is a rifleman." You can only pick a general field. I was bummed out when I found out I didn't get tanks but couldn't be too mad, since I knew it was a possibility.

Q: How did you train for this career?

A: After boot camp and combat training my MOS (military occupational specialty) school took place at Fort Sill, Oklahoma, which is actually an army base. Cannoneer school was around 30 days long and consisted of a combination of classroom instruction and hands-on practical application in the field. We took written tests and had to learn all the different types of ammunition and fuses we use in Artillery and had to become familiar with the ins and outs of the M777A2 howitzer, the cannon we use.

Q: Can you describe a typical workday?

A: A typical day in an artillery battery depends if we are in the field or not. If we are not in the field we usually wake up around 5:00 in the morning and have formation PT [physical training], either as a gun section (roughly eight Marines) or as a platoon (40 Marines). PT can consist of running up the treacherous hills we have here in Camp Pendleton, circuit workouts, or just going to the gym. After PT, I would go back to my room, shower, and change into cammies [camouflage uniform] to make it to 8:00 a.m. formation.

My work area is at the gun park, which is like giant lot with an overhead cover, where the howitzers are kept. We spend the day laying all the gear out and doing maintenance on the gun and "busting rust"—literally! We also do inventory and make sure every piece of the gun is accounted for and see what is broken so we can fix it or replace before the next field op. On an average day we get off around 1630 hours (4:30 p.m.) but sometimes we stay until the work is done, which could be late at night.

In the field is where we can actually perform and train in our job. When we're in the field, we work roughly 20-hour days. We spend our time shooting live ammunition with the howitzer. Field ops can range from a couple of days to a month, depending on what the mission is and how much the command wants to train. There are no showers or bathrooms in the field (Baby wipes become your best friend!) and only MREs to eat. [An MRE is a "meal ready to eat," which is the packaged food for the military.] I personally think MREs taste awful so I pack my own cans of fruit and soup to eat out there. We sleep wherever we stop shooting for the night in between fire missions, right on the ground in the dirt. Since I am also a driver I sometimes sleep in the cab of my seven-ton truck.

Q: What do you like most about your job?

A: I would say the tight-knit brotherhood of the artillery community is what I like best. The people you work with are the only people you have around and can rely on. I also take pride in my job being as difficult and physically demanding as it is. Many Marines I have spoken to in other job fields saw how we operate on the gun line and said they would not want to do what we do because of the brutal conditions we face and the constant stress.

Q: What do you like least about your job?

A: I would have to say the thing I like the least is the wear and tear on my body. I am 23 but feel a lot older some days. Lifting 100-lb. rounds takes it toll on your knees and back after a while.

Q: What personal qualities do you find most valuable for this type of work?

A: Having a thick skin is important in my job and trying to keep an even head when dealing with things that you really do not want to do. I live by the motto "It could always be worse."

Q: What advice do you have for students who might be interested in this career?

A: I would suggest going into a job field where you can actually learn a skill or trade so it can transfer into the civilian sector. Artillery does not offer much in that aspect! But I can't complain too much. I joined the Marine Corps and wanted to do something that I wouldn't be able to do in the civilian world. Well, I got my wish!

Find Out More

Bureau of Labor Statistics
www.bls.gov/ooh/military/military-careers.htm

This website provides information on a variety of military careers, as well as statistics related to salaries and job opportunities.

Marine Corps Community Services (MCCS) Civilian Careers
www.usmc-mccs.org/careers/#.VdDekJd8vwY

The MCCS serves military communities all over the world, providing job information and benefits to military personnel and their families.

Marine Corps Jobs at a Glance
www.military.com/join-armed-forces/Marine-corps-jobs.html

This military-oriented website provides general information on all specialties in the Marines.

Official Website of the US Marine Corps
www.marines.mil

This site features news stories about Marines and their experiences and achievements, along with videos, photos, and other information.

Today's Military
www.todaysmilitary.com

This US Department of Defense site includes information about all branches of the military and provides targeted information for parents, educators, and potential military personnel.

US Marine Corps
www.marines.com

This website includes videos, articles, and much more information about all aspects of life in the corps, from enlistment to becoming an officer and beyond.

Other Jobs in the Marine Corps

Administrative clerk
Aircraft maintenance
Air delivery specialist
Air traffic controller
Ammunition technician
Amphibious vehicle crewman
Aviation ordnance technician
Biological defense specialist
Chemical defense specialist
Combat correspondent
Combat media specialist
Communications
Computer systems specialist
Data network specialist
Electrician
Engineer
Explosive ordnance disposal
Explosive ordnance maintenance
Field artillery
Field radio operator

Ground ordnance disposal
Ground ordnance maintenance
Intelligence analyst
Landing support specialist
Logistics/embarkation specialist
Machine gunner
Machinist
Motor transport
Nuclear defense specialist
Personnel clerk
Pilot
Radar operator
Refrigeration mechanic
Satellite communications
    terminal operator
Supply clerk
Traffic management specialist
Translator
Wireman

Index

Picture Credits

About the Author

Joanne Mattern has written many nonfiction books for young people, including several career guides and profiles. She enjoys making real-life events and issues come to life for her readers. She lives in New York State with her husband, four children, and several pets.